English Language Workshop

Exploring Writing

Workbook 2

Sue Garnett BEd, MA

This edition first published 2002 by
Learners Publishing Pte Ltd
222 Tagore Lane
#03-01 TG Building
Singapore 787603
Email: learnpub@learners.com.sg
Website: http://www.learners.com.sg

by arrangement with R.I.C. Publications Pty Ltd
Perth, Western Australia.

Reprinted 2002, 2003, 2004

ISBN 981 4070 58 0

Printed by Seng Lee Press Pte Ltd, Singapore

LEARNERS PUBLISHING

How to use this book

Each unit consists of four pages with the following features.

Each unit begins with a model of a particular type of fiction or non-fiction text. It can be read orally if required.

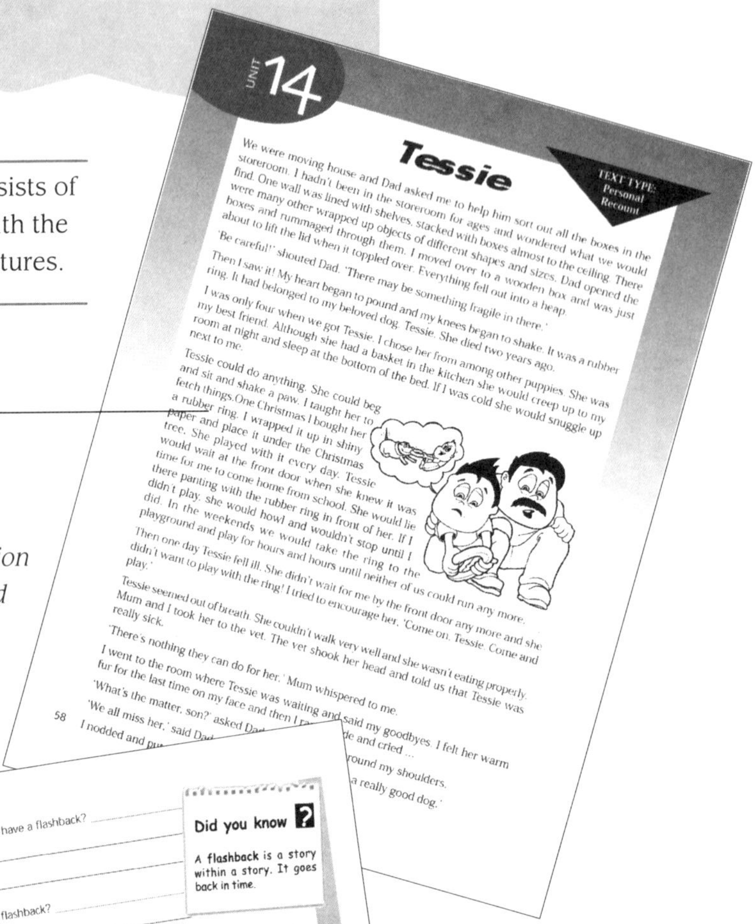

UNIT 14

Tessie

TEXT TYPE: Personal Recount

We were moving house and Dad asked me to help him sort out all the boxes in the storeroom. I hadn't been in the storeroom for ages and wondered what we would find. One wall was lined with shelves, stacked with boxes almost to the ceiling. There were many other wrapped up objects of different shapes and sizes. Dad opened the boxes and rummaged through them. I moved over to a wooden box and was just about to lift the lid when it toppled over. Everything fell out into a heap.

'Be careful!' shouted Dad. 'There may be something fragile in there.'

Then I saw it! My heart began to pound and my knees began to shake. It was a rubber ring. It had belonged to my beloved dog, Tessie. She died two years ago.

I was only four when we got Tessie. I chose her from among other puppies. She was my best friend. Although she had a basket in the kitchen she would creep up to my room at night and sleep at the bottom of the bed. If I was cold she would snuggle up next to me.

Tessie could do anything. She could beg and sit and shake a paw. I taught her to fetch things.One Christmas I bought her a rubber ring. I wrapped it up in shiny paper and place it under the Christmas tree. She played with it every day. Tessie would wait at the front door when she knew it was time for me to come home from school. She would lie there panting with the rubber ring in front of her. If I didn't play, she would howl and wouldn't stop until I did. In the weekends we would take the ring to the playground and play for hours and hours until neither of us could run any more.

Then one day Tessie fell ill. She didn't wait for me by the front door any more and she didn't want to play with the ring! I tried to encourage her. 'Come on, Tessie. Come and play.'

Tessie seemed out of breath. She couldn't walk very well and she wasn't eating properly. Mum and I took her to the vet. The vet shook her head and told us that Tessie was really sick.

'There's nothing they can do for her,' Mum whispered to me.

I went to the room where Tessie was waiting and said my goodbyes. I felt her warm fur for the last time on my face and then I ra... de and cried ...

'What's the matter, son?' asked Dad ... round my shoulders.

'We all miss her,' said Dad ... a really good dog.'

I nodded and pu...

58

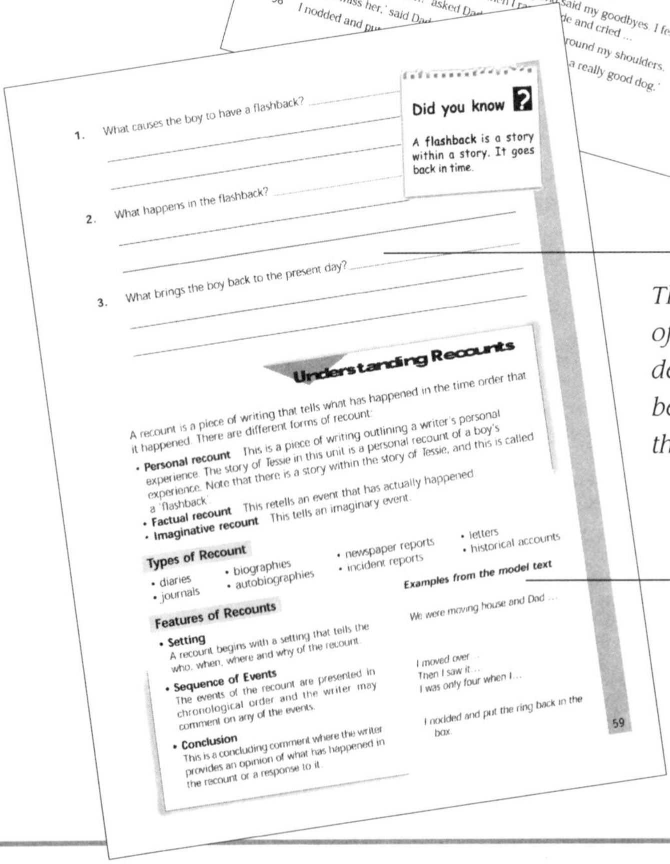

1. What causes the boy to have a flashback?

2. What happens in the flashback?

3. What brings the boy back to the present day?

Did you know ?

A flashback is a story within a story. It goes back in time.

Understanding Recounts

A recount is a piece of writing that tells what has happened in the time order that it happened. There are different forms of recount:

- **Personal recount** This is a piece of writing outlining a writer's personal experience. The story of Tessie in this unit is a personal recount of a boy's experience. Note that there is a story within the story of Tessie, and this is called a 'flashback'.
- **Factual recount** This retells an event that has actually happened.
- **Imaginative recount** This tells an imaginary event.

Types of Recount

- diaries
- journals
- biographies
- autobiographies
- newspaper reports
- incident reports
- letters
- historical accounts

Features of Recounts

Examples from the model text

- **Setting** A recount begins with a setting that tells the who, when, where and why of the recount. — We were moving house and Dad ...
- **Sequence of Events** The events of the recount are presented in chronological order and the writer may comment on any of the events. — I moved over ... Then I saw it ... I was only four when I ...
- **Conclusion** This is a concluding comment where the writer provides an opinion of what has happened in the recount or a response to it. — I nodded and put the ring back in the box.

59

The activities focus on key features of the text type or form. They are designed to promote discussion before students attempt to write their own composition.

Information about the text type of the writing model .

Preface

Exploring Writing Workbook 2 uses a range of fiction and non-fiction texts with activities designed to improve students' writing and comprehension skills. The text types featured in this book range from recounts, brochures and expositions to more unusual forms such as flashbacks and cautionary tales. A clear example of each writing form or text type is provided. This is followed by information about the model text and its features. For the writing assignment, space is provided for students to write preparatory notes before they attempt their own piece of writing in the same genre.

The book aims to help students

- become familiar with some of the ways in which texts can be structured;
- write confidently, fluently and with understanding; and
- develop their power of imagination, inventiveness and critical awareness.

All ideas have been tried and tested in the classroom. They can be used with small groups or whole classes.

Checklist to help students write according to the intended purpose and audience.

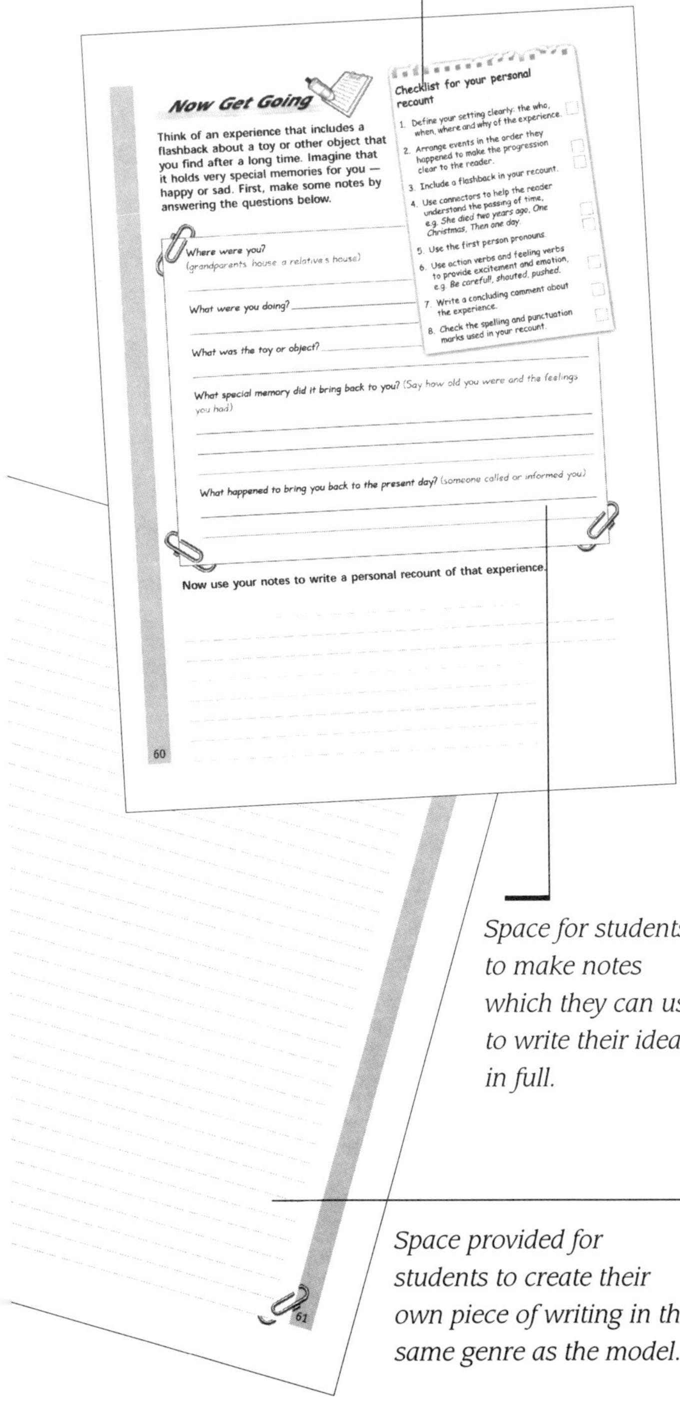

Space for students to make notes which they can use to write their ideas in full.

Space provided for students to create their own piece of writing in the same genre as the model.

Curriculum Links

The activities in this book have been written to encourage students to demonstrate the following learning outcomes.

Learning Outcomes	Language skills, strategies and/or attitudes
Respond to a variety of texts and demonstrate a positive attitude towards reading and language	• Respond creatively and imaginatively to a variety of texts. • Enjoy the creative use of language.
Present and develop ideas effectively in writing for a variety of purposes and audiences	• Plan and organize with purpose and audience in mind. • Select an appropriate focus and format, and develop main ideas that are relevant to the topic or support an opinion on the topic.
Write legibly, coherently and cohesively for different purposes and audiences	• Select the text type that suits the intended purpose. • Support or elaborate on ideas with relevant details. • Use grammar, punctuation and vocabulary appropriately. • Edit a text.
Demonstrate knowledge about language and text types from print sources	• Understand and use appropriately terms relating to text types/forms and literary features. • Understand how the purpose of various text types is achieved through text organization, grammar and vocabulary. • Understand and use grammatical items and structures.
Read and view a variety of texts and demonstrate in written form the ability to acquire and use knowledge for a variety of purposes	• Gather information using search options, e.g. subject and key words. • Give reasons to support a response, point of view or opinion. • Identify and analyse techniques used in achieving a variety of purposes.

Contents

How to use this book 2
Preface 3
Curriculum Links 4

Unit		Page	Text Type/Form	Skills/Strategies
1	**The Easter Bunny**	6	Narrative	Writing for a specific audience
2	**The School Play**	10	Personal Recount	Retelling an event
3	**A Landing Surprise!**	14	Narrative	Continuing a story
4	**White**	18	Description (Poem)	Using descriptive language
5	**The Three Goats**	22	Narrative	Writing from a different point of view
6	**Environment Week**	26	Procedure	Writing in different styles to suit audience
7	**Crocodile on the Loose**	30	Factual Recount	Knowing the features of a news report
8	**The School Canteen**	34	Exposition	Presenting opposing points of view
9	**The Race**	38	Narrative	Writing a modern version of a fable
10	**Daniel Brown**	42	Information Report	Using adjectives and adverbs
11	**Hand-held Computer Games**	46	Exposition	Putting forward an argument
12	**Billy the Bully**	50	Narrative	Writing a cautionary tale
13	**The Skateboard Park**	54	Exposition	Developing supporting facts
14	**Tessie**	58	Personal Recount	Writing a flashback
15	**My Hobby**	62	Information Report	Writing a speech
16	**Does Santa Claus Exist?**	66	Exposition	Explaining one's point of view
17	**Messages and Mummies**	70	Information Report	Writing a synopsis
18	**Visit Wales**	74	Information Report	Writing a brochure

UNIT 1

TEXT TYPE:
Narrative

The Easter Bunny

Each year King Bunny had a competition to see who would be the Easter Bunny and deliver Easter eggs to the children in the village. King Bunny would hide a golden egg and whoever found it would become the Easter Bunny. Bernard Bunny always entered the competition but never won.

'You know why you don't win?' said his mother. 'It's because you don't eat carrots. They help you to see better.'

'But I hate carrots,' Bernard tried to explain.

'Well, you'll never win then, will you?' said his mother.

'I will,' insisted Bernard. 'One day I will.'

One sunny afternoon while Bernard was lying in the meadow, he heard footsteps. Bernard pricked up his ears. He could see two people – they were crawling along the grass looking for something. After a while they walked away, grumbling. Bernard crept to the spot where they had been looking. He looked closer. What was it? There in front of his eyes was a pair of glasses. He put them on and looked around.

'Wow, I can see,' he shouted. 'I can see over the meadow, to the wood and into the town. I can really see.'

The next morning, the rabbits lined up for the competition. Bernard put on his glasses. The other rabbits laughed.

'What are those things you're wearing?' one asked.

'They're glasses,' said Bernard. 'They help me to see.'

'You look silly,' they laughed. 'You've got four eyes.'

'We'll see,' he said, smiling. 'We'll see.'

'Ready, steady, go!' shouted King Bunny.

Bernard ran down to the pond. Suddenly something caught his eye. It was a long way off, but it glinted in the sun just like his gold-edged glasses. He looked again. There in the middle of the pond was a lily pad and in the middle was ... the golden egg. He reached out with a long stick and pulled it in.

King Bunny was amazed. 'Well done, Bernard,' he said. 'What you're wearing looks really useful. Could you get me a pair?'

Well, that was the beginning — not only did Bernard deliver the Easter eggs to the children, but he opened a little shop selling glasses. And who says rabbits don't wear glasses?

Did you know ?

The Easter Bunny is a story written for young children. When you write a story you need to consider the **audience**, i.e. who it is for.

1. Review the story, *The Easter Bunny*. Does it consider the needs of the audience? Look at the points below and tick the ones which you think are true.
   - **a.** Suitable vocabulary for young children to read ☐
   - **b.** Suitable vocabulary for young children to understand ☐
   - **c.** Appropriate sentence structure: simple sentences, few complex sentences ☐
   - **d.** Suitable title ☐
   - **e.** Suitable storyline ☐
   - **f.** Appropriate length ☐
   - **g.** Good presentation ☐
   - **h.** Appropriate illustrations ☐
   - **i.** Suitable ending ☐

2. How could you improve this story to meet the audience's needs better?

___

Understanding Narratives

A narrative text tells an imaginary story although the story may be based on facts. The purpose of a narrative is to entertain the reader.

Types of Narrative

- short stories
- fables
- modern fantasy
- folk tales
- plays
- legends
- myths
- ballads

Features of Narratives

	Examples from the model text
• Orientation This is the beginning of a story. It sets the mood by defining the place and time the story happens, the main characters and other information to give the reader an 'orientation' or starting point.	*Each year King Bunny...*
• Sequence of Events This is the main body of the story and it outlines an event or a sequence of events which leads the characters into a complication, which may be a problem or dilemma, where the normal events are overcome by some form of conflict. The writer may introduce more than one complication so as to frustrate the character/s in achieving their desired outcome. This also builds tension and anticipation in the reader.	*You know why you don't win ...* *'Wow!' he shouted ...*
• Resolution Very often, as in *The Easter Bunny*, everything ends up 'happily ever after' after the conflicts are resolved. In some narratives, the resolution may be left for the reader to decide.	*... he opened a little shop ...*

Now Get Going

Think of a suitable story of your own for young children. Make notes for your story in the space below.

Orientation

Who: ______________________________

What: ______________________________

When: ______________________________

Where: ______________________________

Sequence of Events

Event/Complication 1: ______________________________

Event/Complication 2: ______________________________

Event/Complication 3: ______________________________

Event/Complication 4: ______________________________

Resolution ______________________________

Checklist for your children's story

1. Choose a storyline that suits the audience. ☐
2. Define your main characters clearly. ☐
3. Use suitable vocabulary that young readers can understand. ☐
4. Write in simple sentences or appropriate complex sentences. ☐
5. Write in the past tense, using action verbs and feeling verbs to provide excitement and emotion, e.g. he ***heard*** footsteps..., ***walked*** away, ***grumbling*** ... ☐
6. Use linking words to help the readers understand the passing of time. ☐
7. Use descriptive language, including adjectives and adverbs. ☐
8. Use paragraphs to show separate sections in your story. ☐
9. Give your story a suitable ending and title. ☐
10. Check the spelling and punctuation marks used in your story. ☐

Now write your story for a young audience.

START

UNIT 2

The School Play

TEXT TYPE: Personal Recount

I have many happy memories of primary school, but the one that stands out most in my mind is the play we had three years ago.

Mrs Menon, our class teacher, had written a play of her own version of 'Jack and the Beanstalk'. On a wet Friday after school, she auditioned everyone who wanted to be in the play. I hadn't really wanted to be in it because I couldn't sing, dance or act. However, she caught me on my way out, saying she had just the part for me. She told me to get on all fours and walk across the stage. That was it, I got the part. I was to be Jack's cow! I was to be the front end of the cow and Thomas, my best friend, was the back end.

We didn't have much to do apart from the occasional 'moo' and a gallop across the stage, but we enjoyed the practices, especially as we could munch sweets and pull funny faces without anyone knowing about it.

Soon it was the evening of the performance. I remember Mrs Menon saying, 'Don't let me down.' We didn't let her down, but it didn't turn out as we expected!

In the first scene, Jack sold us for some beans and we went off to our new owner. In Mrs Menon's version of the story, we escaped and ran back home, just in time to see Jack cutting down the beanstalk to stop the giant following him. However, Jack's mum, who had been doing some washing, accidentally spilt too much water on the stage. The caretaker had only that morning waxed the stage without anyone's knowledge and as a result, the stage was exceedingly slippery. Thomas and I flew across the slippery floor and went headfirst into the beanstalk. Then, CHAOS! The beanstalk came tumbling down, followed by the giant who got caught in the washing line. With polka-dot underpants covering his eyes, Billy (the giant) stumbled across the stage and shot off the edge into the audience. The audience were in hysterics, clapping and cheering with sheer delight.

We received a standing ovation and our picture appeared in the local newspaper. And as for Mrs Menon, she left teaching and went into theatre. However, I believe she won't work with animals or children!

1. List the events that led to the giant falling off the stage.

____

____

____

____

2. Why do you think this is a happy memory for the writer?

____

____

____

____

3. Would you describe the play as a success? Why?

____

____

____

____

____

Understanding Recounts

A recount is a piece of writing which retells something that actually happened. There are different forms of recount:

- A **personal recount** retells a writer's personal experience. *The School Play* in this unit is an example of a personal recount.
- A **factual recount** retells the happenings of an actual event.
- An **imaginative recount** tells an imaginary event.

Types of Recount

- diaries
- journals
- letters
- historical accounts
- newspaper reports
- incident reports
- autobiographies
- biographies

Features of Recounts

Examples from the model text

- **Setting**
  This is the beginning of a recount and it tells the who, when, where and why of something that has happened.
  I have many happy memories...
- **Sequence of Events**
  The events of a recount are presented in chronological order and the writer may comment on any of the events.
  ... after school ...
  Soon it was evening...
  In the first scene ...
- **Conclusion**
  This is a closing comment where the writer provides an opinion of what has happened in the recount.
  ...I believe she won't work with animals or children.

Now Get Going

What special memories do you have of school? Choose one you remember most vividly and make notes of the account in the space below.

Checklist for your personal recount

1. Define your setting clearly. ☐
2. Arrange the events in the order they happened to make the progression clear to the reader. ☐
3. Use linking words to help the reader understand the passing of time . ☐
4. Use the first personal pronouns, e.g. *I, we*. ☐
5. Use action verbs and feeling verbs to provide excitement and emotion. ☐
6. Vary the length of your sentences to create effect. ☐
7. Use paragraphs to show separate sections in your story. ☐
8. Write a concluding comment on the experience. ☐
9. Check the spelling and punctuation marks used in your recount. ☐

Setting

____

____

____

____

Sequence of Events

Event 1: ______________________________

____

Event 2: ______________________________

____

Event 3: ______________________________

____

Event 4: ______________________________

____

Conclusion (*What happened at the end?*)

____

____

Now write the account in detail for an unknown reader, using the notes you made.

____

____

____

____

____

____

____

UNIT 3

TEXT TYPE:
Narrative
(Science Fiction)

A Landing Surprise!

EPISODE 1

Star Date: 2976

Starship *Breaker* circled the planet Ogg, looking for a suitable place to land and explore the planet.

'Is it safe to land?' asked Captain Phantos.

'Absolutely,' replied Commander Ramesh. 'There have been no UFO sightings here.'

'Are you sure?' the captain asked, worriedly. 'There's something strange about this planet. I think we should head back to base.'

'Don't worry,' reassured the commander. 'It is safe to land here.'

Starship *Breaker* circled the planet again, its green laser lighting up the surface. The crew beamed down to the planet's surface. Commander Ramesh watched as they disappeared. They were in safe hands; it was the captain's tenth mission. After a while, Commander Ramesh shut his eyes and dreamt about returning home to Planet Zoiteck.

He was woken by a loud crash; the ship began to tilt and the buzzers flashed and beeped: 'DANGER. RED ALERT. UFO in close proximity!'

Commander Ramesh jumped to his feet and looked at the screen. Swarms of UFOs were circling the planet.

'Teleport back to base!' he shouted. 'Now!'

'We can't, there's no power,' answered Captain Phantos on his wrist communicator.

'I'll come and get you!' shouted the commander, turning the ship around and heading in the direction of Ogg.

Another missile hit the ship rocking it from side to side. Commander Ramesh fell forward and hit the control panel. In a daze, he watched the screen flicker before his eyes.

A voice echoed around the control room. 'PREPARE FOR YOUR DOOM!' the voice crackled.

A red mist circled the ship and then ... BOOM!

1. How do you know this is a science fiction story?

____

____

2. a. The writer uses lots of verbs in the story. List some of them.

____

b. Why has the writer used these verbs? ______________________

____

3. a. Who are the characters? ______________________

b. What is the setting for the story? ______________________

____

c. What is the plot? ______________________

____

d. What is the ending of the episode? ______________________

____

Understanding Narratives

A narrative text tells an imaginary story although the story may be based on facts. The purpose of a narrative is to entertain the reader. The narrative text in this unit, *A Landing Surprise!* is a science fiction story.

Types of Narrative

- short stories
- fables
- modern fantasy
- folk tales
- plays
- legends
- myths
- science fiction

Features of Narratives

Examples from the model text

- **Orientation**
  A narrative begins with an orientation which sets the mood of the story. It defines the place, time, main character/s and other information to give the reader an 'orientation' or starting point.

  Star Date: 2976, Starship ***Breaker*** *circled the planet Ogg....*

- **Sequence of Events**
  This is the main body of the story. It describes an event or a sequence of events which leads the character/s into a complication where the normal events are overcome by some form of conflict. Very often, more than one complication is created to frustrate the character/s in achieving their desired outcome. It also serves to build tension and anticipation in the reader.

  ... Is it safe to land? ...
  ... woken up by a loud crash ...
  A voice echoed ...

- **Resolution**
  Everything ends up 'happily ever after' after the conflicts are resolved. However, some narratives may not end happily. In some other narratives, such as *A Landing Surprise!* in this unit, the resolution may be left for the reader to decide.

  ... and then ...Boom!

Now Get Going

Imagine that the story of Starship *Breaker* continues. What happens to Captain Phantos and his crew? Make some notes for Episode 2 of the story.

Checklist for your Episode 2

1. Begin with a description of Captain Phantos and his crew. ☐
2. Use the same language and vocabulary as in Episode 1. ☐
3. Use linking words to help the reader understand the passing of time, e.g. *after a while..., circled the planet again....* ☐
4. Use descriptive language, including adjectives and adverbs to provide a clear picture in the reader's mind. ☐
5. Use lots of action verbs and feeling verbs to provide excitement and emotion, e.g. *head back, flashed and beeped, crackled.* ☐
6. Use paragraphs to show separate sections in your story. ☐
7. Give a suitable title to your Episode2. ☐
8. Check the spelling and punctuation marks used in your narrative. ☐

EPISODE 2

Characters ______________________

____

____

Setting *(where do they end in Episode 1)* ______________________

____

____

Plot *(what happens to the characters?)* ______________________

____

____

____

____

____

____

Ending ______________________

____

Now write Episode 2, using the notes you made.

UNIT 4

TEXT TYPE:
Description
(Poem)

White

White are the clouds
You see on a hot summer's day,
White are the snowflakes
Which swirl and twirl across the sky,
White is vanilla ice-cream
Cool and sweet,
White are the pearly white teeth
When small children smile,
White is a swan
Gliding gracefully on the village pond,
White are the bony skeletons
You see on Halloween,
White is the blossom
On trees in the park,
White is the polar bear
Majestic and strong,
White is the dove
The sign of peace.

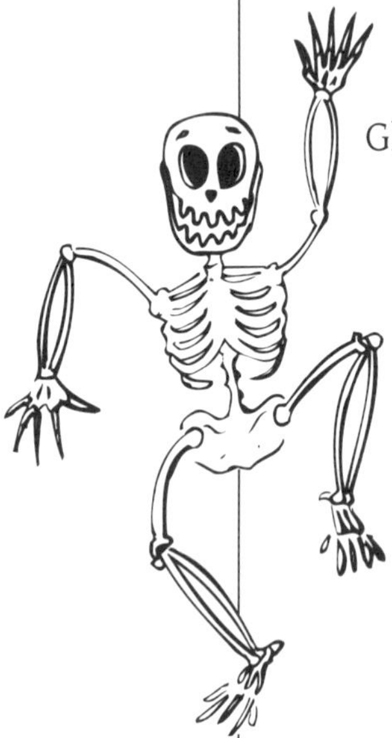

1. List the things that are white in the poem. ______________________________

____

____

____

2. If you are going to extend this poem by two more lines, what would you write?

____

____

3. Complete the table below with appropriate nouns and description from the poem.

Things that are white	Description
clouds	a hot summer's day

Did you know ?

The description of each noun has an important part in making the poem come to life. You can use adjectives and adverbs to bring your poem alive.

Understanding Description Texts

A description is a piece of writing that describes a living or non-living thing. A description can be a specific piece of text or be included in a larger piece of writing, such as a report. In this unit, the description is of the colour *White* and it is written in the form of a poem.

Types of Description

While a description is not always recognized as a specific text type, it is considered an important writing skill. It is necessary to learn how to write accurate descriptions as part of many other forms of text type.

Features of Descriptions

Examples from the model text

- **Introduction**
  The beginning introduces who or what is being described.
  White (heading of the poem)
- **Description**
  This explores the features of the object, person or animal, such as its appearance, behaviours, habits, qualities, uses, etc.
  White are the clouds
  White is vanilla ice-cream
- **Special Features**
  These include the description of special and unique features of the object, person or animal.
  majestic and strong…
  gliding gracefully
- **Conclusion**
  This is a concluding statement that may be a fact or an opinion.
  The sign of peace.

Now Get Going

Make some notes in the space below for your poem on a colour of your choice.

Checklist for your description

1. Use a variety of adjectives that suit the selected colour. ☐
2. Focus on the features of the colour, physical and non-physical, e.g. *snowflakes, sign of peace.* ☐
3. Use figurative language, including similes and metaphors, to create a vivid picture in your reader's mind, e.g. *swirl and twirl, majestic and strong.* ☐
4. Give a title to your poem. ☐
5. Check the spelling and punctuation marks used in your poem. ☐

Introduction

Colour: ______________________

Description/Special Features

Nouns	*Description*
____________	______________________
____________	______________________
____________	______________________
____________	______________________
____________	______________________
____________	______________________
____________	______________________
____________	______________________
____________	______________________
____________	______________________
____________	______________________

Conclusion ______________________

Now write your poem in the space below.

UNIT 5

TEXT TYPE: Narrative

The Three Goats

My name is Wolf. I'm in bed, feeling miserable with bad burns on my paws. You might ask why. Well, it all happened one warm summer's day when I woke up sneezing. I thought that I have got a cold and went to the doctor's. He told me it was hay fever and that I should stay indoors until summer was over. When I got home, there was a message on my answering machine. My mother was ill, so I decided to visit her and cheer her up.

As I was walking along, I came across a new house made of straw. I could see a little goat at the front of the house doing the finishing touches. Just as I was about to say 'hello', I felt a sneeze coming on: 'Atishoo'

The house of straw blew away. I was stunned and before I could say 'sorry' to the little goat, he dashed off down the lane. Running after him, I tried to tell him it was an accident.

Then we came to a house of sticks. A little goat was at the front door adding the finishing touches to his new house. I was just about to say what a lovely house he had when I felt another sneeze coming on: 'Atishoo!'

The house of sticks fell down with a crash. I was about to say how sorry I was, then the little goats ran off down the lane, squealing. I followed them until we came to a house of bricks. The goats rushed inside and shut the door with a bang. I knocked at the door trying to explain what had happened but they wouldn't let me in.

Then I sneezed again so hard that my cap blew off and it landed on the chimney. It was my favourite cap, so I climbed up onto the roof to get it. I was just about to grab hold of the cap when I sneezed again and the cap slipped down the chimney. I decided that the only thing I could do was climb down and get it. Splash! I fell into a pot of boiling water! That's why I'm sitting in bed now wrapped in bandages. Next year when I get hay fever, I'll stay inside all summer—that's definite!

1. **a.** Does the story above remind you of any story that you have read or heard before? Give the title of the story.

____

b. What is the difference between that story and the one above?

____

____

2. Do you think that this is a believable version of that story? ____________

Why? ____

Understanding Narratives

A narrative text tells an imaginary story although the story may be based on facts. *The Three Goats* is written as an alternative version of a well-known children's story. The purpose of a narrative is to entertain the reader.

Types of Narrative

- short stories
- fables
- modern fantasy
- folk tales
- plays
- legends
- myths
- ballads

Features of Narratives

Examples from the model text

- **Orientation**
  A narrative begins with an orientation which sets the mood of the story. It defines the place, time, main character/s and other information to give the reader an 'orientation' or starting point.

  My name is Wolf ...

- **Sequence of Events**
  This is the main body of the story. It describes an event or a sequence of events which leads the character/s into a complication, which can be a problem or dilemma, where the normal events are overcome by some form of conflict. Very often, more than one complication is created to frustrate the character/s in achieving their desired outcome. It also serves to build tension and anticipation in the reader.

  ... there was a message ...
  ... before I could say 'sorry' ...
  Then I sneezed again ...

- **Resolution**
  Everything ends up 'happily ever after' after the conflicts are resolved. However, some narratives may not end happily as in the case of the wolf in this story of *The Three Goats*. In some other narratives, the resolution may be left for the reader to decide.

  ... Next year, when I get hay fever ...

Now Get Going

Do you remember the story of Red Riding Hood? Imagine you are the wolf in the story and that you are in no way to blame for what happened to her Grandma. Answer these questions in note form, thinking of the excuses for your actions.

Checklist for your narrative

1. Define the setting and your main characters clearly. ☐
2. Use the first person pronouns, e.g. *I, me*. ☐
3. Write in the past tense - the story has already happened! ☐
4. Use linking words to help the reader understand the passing of time, e.g. *when I got home..., as I was walking....* ☐
5. Use descriptive language, including adjectives and adverbs, to provide a clear picture in the reader's mind, e.g. *miserable, with a bang, so hard.* ☐
6. Use action verbs and feeling verbs to provide excitement and emotion, e.g. *dashed, squealing, hate.* ☐
7. Use paragraphs to show separate sections in your story. ☐
8. Check the spelling and punctuation marks used in your story. ☐

- Why did you follow Red Riding Hood?

  ____

  ____

- Why did you go into her Grandma's house?

  ____

  ____

- How did Grandma end up in the cupboard?

  ____

- Why did you put on Grandma's clothes?

  ____

- Why did you jump out of bed and chase Red Riding Hood?

  ____

  ____

Now write the story of Red Riding Hood explaining what happened from the wolf's point of view.

UNIT 6

TEXT TYPE: Procedure

Environment Week

A teacher informed the students in his class about what was happening during Environment Week. He asked them to take notes. Here are the notes taken by Tom.

Envir. Wk. Trees

Mon. visit woods, lunch, boots, caps

Tues. tree planting p.m., boots, gloves, ask Dad for a spade

Wed. slide show on forests 9.30 a.m.

Thurs. a.m. visit library

Fri. projects in hall, 9-11 a.m. tell Mum and Dad to come

The teacher asked Tom to convert his notes into an itinerary for the rest of the class to take home. This is what he wrote.

Itinerary for Environment Week

Focus: Trees

Monday Full-day visit to Sunnybank Woods.
Packed lunch necessary.
Suitable clothing and footwear required.

Tuesday Afternoon tree planting, appropriate footwear.
Tools needed e.g. spades, forks.

Wednesday Slide show at 9.30 a.m. on Forests of the World.

Thursday Visit to the town library in the morning.

Friday Projects exhibition from 9.00 a.m. to 11.00 a.m.
Parents welcome.

1. What do you think an itinerary is? ______________________________

____

2. Look at Tom's two sets of notes above. Make a comparison between them by completing the table below.

	First Note	***Second Note***
Style	*informal*	
Words		
Presentation		

Did you know ?

When Tom wrote his second set of notes, he had to take into consideration the audience that would be reading it. This made a difference to his style, the words he used and the presentation.

3. Which of Tom's notes would be useful to only him? ______________________

Why? ____

____

____

4. Which would be useful to both himself and the rest of the class? ____________

Why? ____

____

____

Understanding Procedures

A procedure is a passage of writing which outlines how something is done. In this unit, the procedure is in the form of an itinerary describing how *Environment Week* would occur.

Types of Procedure

- recipes
- instruction manuals
- science experiments
- itineraries
- messages

Features of Procedures

	Examples from the model text
Procedures traditionally contain the following features but due to their wide usage, the features can vary.	
• **Aim** The opening statement states what has to be done in order for the procedure to be successful. It usually emphasizes that the procedure must be followed for the aim to be successful.	*Itinerary for Environment Week*
• **Materials** This is a listing of all the materials needed to carry out the procedure effectively.	*lunch, boots, caps ...*
• **Method** The method is presented in a series of steps or things to do. In this unit, the *Itinerary for Environment Week* presents the order of things to do on each day of the Environment Week.	*Monday, Tuesday, ...*
Note that in the model text for procedure in this unit, the materials and method are presented together as they differ for each day of the week.	

Now Get Going

Imagine your teacher gives you the following information.

Next week is Book Week,
and we wilL be doing several activities.

On Monday, we will be visited by children's author Jack Shaw. He will be reading to us from his latest book and giving us writing tips. On Tuesday and Wednesday, we will be making our own class book of stories to present to a younger class at the end of the week. On Thursday, we will visit the Children's Literature Centre. You will need to bring your lunch. The bus leaves at 9 a.m. from the front of the school. On Friday from 9 to 11 a.m, we will be reading our book of stories to the younger class.

Checklist for your itinerary

1. State the aim/focus of the itinerary. ☐
2 Make the style of presentation suit the audience. ☐
3. Use vocabulary appropriate to the audience. ☐
4. Use abbreviated sentences where possible, without reducing the details needed. ☐
5. Include details on time and key information accurately. ☐
6. Check the spelling and punctuation marks used in your itinerary. ☐

Use the teacher's information on Book Week to make some notes in the space below.

Aim/Focus ______________________________

Day	Activity
____________	______________________________
____________	______________________________
____________	______________________________
____________	______________________________
____________	______________________________
____________	______________________________
____________	______________________________
____________	______________________________
____________	______________________________
____________	______________________________
____________	______________________________
____________	______________________________
____________	______________________________
____________	______________________________

Convert the notes for Book Week into an itinerary which the whole class can use.

UNIT 7

TEXT TYPE: Factual Recount

Crocodile on the Loose!

Adam Razak

JURONGVALE – On Friday, the Emergency Services were called to Riverton Secondary School in Jurongvale, when an escaped crocodile wreaked havoc in the school compound.

The principal, Mrs Angela Bloom, said, 'The secretary told me there was a crocodile in the school compound eating the students' lunches. I ran outside with the caretaker. The students' were, of course, very frightened.'

Mr Chen, the gardener, was quick to act. He used a large broom to push the crocodile into a nearby shed. The students were evacuated quickly without anyone being hurt.

Within minutes the Emergency Services arrived. The crocodile was found to belong to the Wildlife Park. The Park Manager, Mr Fred Kumar, was very apologetic. 'I'm glad that none of the students were hurt,' he said. 'We have invited them to come and visit the park free of charge.'

1. When reporters write a news story they think about the following 4 Ws. Find the facts to the four questions from the above news report.

Who? ______________________

When? ______________________

Where? ______________________

What? ______________________

____

2. A news report usually includes a quote from someone involved in the incident, or a witness. Write one of the quotes from the report.

____

____

____

____

3. Think of some interesting things that could happen at your school. Write some imaginary headlines,

e.g. **SOCCER STAR GIVES OUT AWARDS**

Did you know ?

A news report usually has a headline to attract readers' attention.

Understanding Recounts

A recount is a piece of writing that tells what has happened in the time order that it happened. There are different forms of recount:

- **Personal recount** This is a piece of writing that retells a writer's personal experience.
- **Factual recount** This retells an event that has actually happened. In this unit, *Crocodile on the Loose!* is a factual recount written in the form of a newspaper report.
- **Imaginative recount** This tells an imaginary event.

Types of Recount

- diaries
- journals
- biographies
- autobiographies
- newspaper reports
- incident reports
- letters
- historical accounts

Features of Recounts

Examples from the model text

- **Setting**
  A recount begins with a setting that tells the who, when, where and why of something that has happened.
  On Friday, ...
- **Sequence of Events**
  The events of the recount are presented in chronological order and the writer may comment on any of the events. The newspaper report in this unit also includes quotes from some people involved in the incident, e.g. the Principal and Park Manager.
  The secretary told me...
  ... none of the students were hurt.
- **Conclusion**
  This is a concluding comment where the writer provides an opinion of what has happened. The conclusion can also be a response from someone involved in the incident, e.g. the Park Manager in the newspaper report in this unit.
  ...We have invited them to come and visit the park...

Now Get Going

Choose the headline you like best from Question 3 and write notes for a newspaper report in the space below.

Checklist for your newspaper report

1. Define the setting clearly: the who, when, where and why. ☐
2. Arrange the events in the order they happened to make the progression clear to the reader. ☐
3. Use connectors to help the reader understand the passing of time. ☐
4. Include at least one quote from someone involved in the incident. ☐
5. Write a headline for the report. ☐
6. Check the spelling and punctuation marks used in your report. ☐

Headline ______________________

Who? ______________________

____

Where? ______________________

____

When? ______________________

____

What? ______________________

____

Quotes *(what somebody said)* ______________________

____

____

____

____

Now write your newspaper report here.

UNIT 8

TEXT TYPE: Exposition

The School Canteen

The Principal of Eden Hill High School has asked the School Council to look at the issue of continuing to run the school canteen. The council has interviewed many students, teachers and parents and summarized the views for and against below.

For

- *Students enjoy the canteen lunches*
- *Saves parents from always making lunches*
- *Profits help provide extra school resources*
- *Many healthy snacks and meals are available*
- *Older students enjoy filling in on duty roster when necessary*
- *Helps students' understanding of practical money problems*

Against

- *Ice-cream wrappers and popsticks litter school compound*
- *Expense for parents—feel pressure by children to buy lunch more often than they can afford*
- *Too many students buying ice-creams etc. instead of healthy food*
- *Difficult to find parents at times to volunteer to be on roster*

1. Several people were asked their views about the school canteen. Which of the points above would these people be concerned with?

a. Students ______________________________

____

b. Parents ______________________________

____

c. School nurse ______________________________

____

d. Cleaners ______________________________

____

e. School Canteen Manager ______________________________

____

2. Do you think the canteen at Eden Hill High School will remain open, or be closed? Give reasons for your answer.

____

____

____

____

____

____

____

Understanding Expositions

An exposition explores and evaluates an issue. It presents arguments for and against the issue to convince the reader of a position. In this unit, the exposition explores the arguments for and against the running of a school canteen.

An exposition relies on the logical presentation of facts and can be written to:
- persuade the reader of the writer's point of view;
- present the pros and cons of an issue in order to convince the reader of the writer's point of view; and
- present the pros and cons of an issue to allow the reader to reach a logical conclusion.

When used in an advertisement, the exposition takes only one point of view as the argument against does not serve the advertisment's aim of encouraging people to buy the product.

Types of Exposition

- reviews
- debates
- advertisements

Features of Expositions

Examples from the model text

- **Introduction**
  The introduction presents the issue in the form of an opening statement or headline.
  ... has asked the School Council to look at the issue of...
- **Argument**
  The points for and against the issue are presented with the arguments for the issue presented first.
- **Conclusion**
  The writer may draw a conclusion or restate the position to assist the reader in making up their mind.

Now Get Going

Imagine you are a member of the School Council. The Principal has asked you to look into the issue of riding bicycles to school. Make notes on different people's opposing views on the issue in the space below.

Checklist for your balanced report

1. State the issue as a title for your report. ☐
2. Present the arguments for the issue first. ☐
3. Present the opposing views clearly. ☐
4. Take into consideration the concerns or viewpoints of the different people you interviewed, e.g. the students, parents, teachers. ☐
5. Draw a conclusion on the issue. ☐
6. Check the spelling and punctuation marks used in your writing. ☐

Arguments For

____

____

____

____

Arguments Against

____

____

____

____

Viewpoints of different people concerned with the issue

- ______________________________

  ____
- ______________________________

  ____
- ______________________________

  ____

Now use the notes to write a balanced report summarizing the opposing views.

____

____

____

____

____

____

____

UNIT 9

TEXT TYPE: Narrative

The Race

It was the holidays and the children of Tortown were having a great time at the playground.

'I bet I could beat any of you in a running race,' said Henry, a tall slim boy, kicking stones across the playground.

The other boys looked up at him. They know he was a fast runner; he was also a bighead!

'Go on, I challenge anyone to a race,' Henry said arrogantly.

The boys shook their heads; he was far too fast for any one of them.

'Okay, I'll race you,' said Tom, a small plump boy with rosy cheeks.

The other boys looked up in amazement.

'You can't beat me,' snapped Henry. 'You're far too slow.'

'I can try,' insisted Tom, tucking into his second bar of chocolate.

'Right then,' said Henry. 'Tomorrow, here, at eleven o'clock!'

The next morning the two boys lined up at the starting point.

'On your marks, get set, GO!'

The two boys set off across the playground to the park. As expected, Henry took the lead immediately. When he could no longer see Tom, he began to slow down. It was a hot day and the sun was beating down furiously.

'I might as well have a rest,' he thought. 'If Tom overtakes me, I can always catch up and still win the race.'

So Henry lay down on the grass and fell asleep under a shady tree.

Meanwhile, Tom plodded on very slowly. Taking his time, he eventually got to the park where Henry was sleeping. Quietly he crept past him so as not to wake him. Step by step he neared the finishing line.

Suddenly Henry woke up and jumped to his feet. He started to run and looked back for any sight of Tom, but he wasn't there. Henry ran as fast as he could to the finishing line, but it was too late.

Tom got to the finishing line in plenty of time. The boys clapped and cheered. In the distance they could see Henry sprinting towards them. But it was too late, Tom had already won the race!

Moral of the story:
Slow and steady wins the race!

Aesop was a writer well-known for his stories with a moral. The above story is based on one of his fables.

1. How do we know that *The Race* is a modern version of Aesop's *The Hare and the Tortoise*?

____

____

2. Explain the moral of the story. ______________________________

____

3. Another of Aesop's fables is *The Boy Who Cried Wolf*, which is about a shepherd boy who lied about a wolf coming to kill the sheep. Write a modern version of the story. Imagine it is set in a school and is about a child who tells lies. Think of a few lies he or she could tell, e.g. telling the teacher that the dog chewed his or her homework.

____

____

____

Understanding Narratives

A narrative text tells an imaginary story although the story may be based on facts. In this unit, *The Race* is a narrative written as a modern representation of a fable 'The Hare and the Tortoise' by Aesop. The purpose of a narrative is to entertain the reader.

Types of Narrative

- short stories
- fables
- modern fantasy
- folk tales
- plays
- legends
- myths
- ballads

Features of Narratives

Examples from the model text

- **Orientation**
  A narrative begins with an orientation, which sets the mood of the story. It defines the place, time, main character/s and other information to give the reader an 'orientation' or starting point of the story.

  It was holidays and the children of Tortown...

- **Sequence of Events**
  The main body of the story describes an event or a sequence of events which leads the character/s into a complication where the normal events are overcome by some form of conflict. There may be more than one complication and this serves to frustrate the character/s in achieving their desired outcome. This also aims to build tension and anticipation in the reader.

  Go on, I challenge anyone to a race...
  Okay I'll race...

- **Resolution**
  Everything ends up 'happily ever after' after the conflicts are resolved. In some narratives, the resolution may be left for the reader to decide.

  But it was too late, Tom had...

Now Get Going

Choose one of the ideas you have written for (3) and write notes for your story, following the same plot as the original one. Set the story in modern times.

THE BOY WHO CRIED WOLF	YOUR MODERN VERSION OF THE STORY
Orientation	
Who: shepherd boy, villagers	
What: told lies	
When: while looking after sheep	
Where: in a village	
Sequence of Events	
Complication 1: Shepherd boy lied there was wolf	
Complication 2: Villagers rushed up the hill but saw no wolf	
Complication 3: Boy kept lying; villagers kept coming to save him	
Complication 4: A real wolf came ...	
Resolution: (Moral of the story)	

Checklist for your narrative

1. Define the setting and your main characters clearly. ☐
2. Write in the past tense, using action verbs and feeling verbs to provide excitement and emotion. ☐
3. Use linking words to help the reader understand the passing of time. ☐
4. Use descriptive language, including adjectives and adverbs. ☐
5. Vary the length of your sentences to create effect. ☐
6. Use paragraphs to show separate sections in your story. ☐
7. Conclude with a moral for your story. ☐
8. Check the spelling and punctuation marks used in your narrative. ☐

Write the complete story, and give it a suitable title.

UNIT 10

TEXT TYPE: Information Report

Daniel Brown

SCHOOL REPORT

Student's Name: Daniel Brown **Class:** 2B

SUBJECTS

English

Daniel speaks fluently and with confidence. He listens well to others in class discussions. Daniel understands what he reads as he continues to improve in his reading. He enjoys writing, with lots of ideas for his stories and writing assignments. He is good in his choice of vocabulary and his grammar is sound, but he makes careless spelling mistakes.

Mathematics

Daniel has achieved satisfactory results in Maths. His understanding of mathematical concepts is sound and he is mentally quick. He only makes mistakes when he rushes through his work. However, he does need help with written problems, and he continues to make mistakes in problem work because he is not careful enough in reading the questions.

Science

Daniel has a good general science knowledge and is able to retain all he is taught. He works well with others in group projects. He enjoys investigating and solving problems, so he is usually quick to complete his practical assignments. However, he does not always finish his written work and does not put enough effort in the presentation of his written work.

PERSONAL AND SOCIAL

Daniel has matured this year, relating well with both his peers and teachers. He is a friendly and pleasant member of the class, with a lot to offer even though this is not always apparent. I am sure that with a little more effort and concentration, Daniel will do well at his new school.

1. a. Is this report written in the first person or the third person? ______________

   b. Who do you think wrote this report? ______________

   c. Who is the audience of this report? ______________

2. Highlight the adjectives in green and the adverbs in blue.

3. Find the conjunctions and underline them.

4. Many adjectives and adverbs are found in report writing. Write the words you highlighted in the report on page 42 under the correct headings. Add some more words of your own.

> **Did you know ?**
> A variety of adjectives and adverbs are used in the school report. Also, conjunctions are used to link the clauses.

Positive adjectives and adverbs		Negative adjectives and adverbs	
______	______	______	______
______	______	______	______
______	______	______	______
______	______	______	______
______	______	______	______
______	______	______	______
______	______	______	______
______	______	______	______

Understanding Information Reports

An information report is a piece of writing which presents information about a person, an object, or a place. *Daniel Brown* is a report giving information about a student.

Types of Information Report

- reference articles
- scientific articles
- reports
- text books
- speeches
- lectures

Although reports such as newspaper or eyewitness reports are often identified as information reports, they are more accurately described as recounts as they retell incidents that have happened.

Features of Information Reports

Examples from the model text

- **Classification**
  The opening statement classifies the subject of the report. — *School Report*
- **Description**
  This describes the various aspects of the topic in varying levels of detail. — *Daniel speaks fluently ...* / *... he makes careless spelling mistakes ...*
- **Conclusion**
  A concluding comment can complete a report but it may not always be the case, such as in this report on *Daniel Brown*.

Now Get Going

Imagine you are a teacher and are writing your year-end school report for a student. Make some notes using the headings in the space below.

Checklist for your school report

1. Start with a title or statement to classify your report, e.g. *School Report* ☐
2. Use a variety of adjectives and adverbs to describe the nouns and verbs respectively, e.g. *pleasant, careless, with confidence.* ☐
3. Use conjunctions to link clauses, e.g. *but, however.* ☐
4. Check the spelling and punctuation marks used in your report. ☐

Name ______________________

____

Subjects ______________________

____

____

____

____

Personal and Social ______________________

____

____

____

____

Now write out your report in full based on the notes you made.

REPORT

UNIT 11

TEXT TYPE: Exposition

Hand-held Computer Games

My name is Thomas Park. I attend Seaview High School. I am firmly of the opinion that hand-held computer games should not be banned from schools.

Firstly, if they were banned, just imagine how many unhappy and lonely teenagers there would be. You can play with hand-held computer games at recess with your friends. Moreover, they can help you make new friends. So, the games encourage students to mix with one another.

Secondly, hand-held computer games don't interfere with our schoolwork. Yes, occasionally students would get caught playing with them in class. However, if there are proper rules and punishments, this can be kept under control.

Lastly, these games develop our hand–eye coordination. They are quiet and so are not distracting! Therefore, I can't see why teachers would object to this!

My argument is conclusive: hand-held computers at school are harmless. Moreover, they are fun, help you make friends, can be controlled, and are good for us. Therefore, DON'T BAN HAND-HELD COMPUTER GAMES.

1. What is Thomas's point of view?

   ____

2. Each of the following three paragraphs has a main idea. Write the main idea of each.

   Paragraph 2: ______________________________

   ____

   Paragraph 3: ______________________________

   ____

   Paragraph 4: ______________________________

   ____

3. Imagine you disagree with Thomas. Choose one of his reasons or main ideas and write a reason why you would not agree with it (even if you really do!).

Thomas's reason	Why I disagree

Did you know ?

Certain words can be used to develop the argument and move it forward, e.g. therefore, nevertheless, consequently, as a result, however, moreover.

Understanding Expositions

An exposition explores and evaluates an issue. It presents arguments for and against the issue to convince the reader of a position. In this unit, Thomas Park has presented a point of view and the writing activity requires you to present the opposing point of view. An exposition relies on the logical presentation of facts and can be written:

- to persuade the reader to agree with the writer's point of view;
- to present the pros and cons of an issue in order to convince the reader of the writer's point of view; and
- to present the pros and cons of an issue to allow the reader to reach a logical conclusion.

Note that when used in an advertisement, the exposition presents only one point of view as the argument against will defeat the purpose of convincing people to buy the product.

Types of Exposition

- reviews
- debates
- speeches
- advertisements

Features of Expositions

	Examples from the model text
• **Introduction** This is an opening statement or headline to present the issue clearly.	*I am firmly of the opinion...*
• **Argument** The main body presents the reasons for and against the issue, with the arguments for the issue presented first.	*Firstly, if they were banned...* *Lastly, these games...*
• **Conclusion** The writer may draw a conclusion or restate his or her position to assist the reader in making up their mind.	*My argument is conclusive...*

Now Get Going

Write notes for a teenagers' news programme arguing that hand-held computer games should be banned. Try to think of three to four reasons to support your argument.

Checklist for your persuasive text

1. State your stand clearly in the opening paragraph, e.g. *I am firmly of the opinion....* ☐
2. Show a good knowledge of your issue and position. ☐
3. Use separate paragraphs to present each supporting reason. ☐
4. Use the correct tense to suit the situation. It may vary according to the issue. ☐
5. Use connectors to develop and move your argument forward, e.g. *Firstly, As a result, however.* ☐
6. Restate your position in the concluding paragraph. ☐
7. Check the spelling and punctuation marks used in your argument. ☐

Reasons for banning hand-held computer games

____

____

____

Now use the notes to write your argument.

____

____

UNIT 12

TEXT TYPE:
Narrative

Billy the Bully

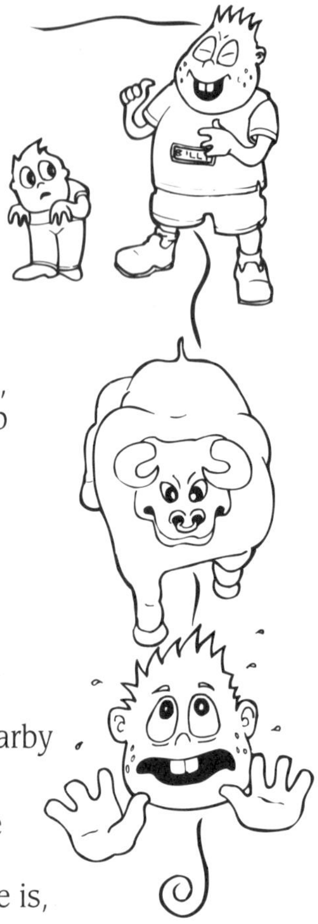

Billy was a bully
The worst in all the school,
He terrorized the children
And broke all of the rules.

Billy was a big lad
Much bigger than the rest,
No-one liked to play with him,
He really was a pest.

He teased some of the children
Laughed and called them names,
'Come over here you little shrimp
And let me play your game.'

The children were so frightened
They didn't know what to do,
They said, 'Billy you're a bully,
We've had enough of you.'

Then a dreadful thing happened
On a day trip to the farm,
They saw a large bull in the field nearby
Said Bill, 'I'll come to no harm.'

Billy jumped right over the fence
'A bullfighter I will be,
Just look at that bull, what a softy he is,
I'm sure he's frightened of me.'

Billy waved his red hanky
All the children could do was stare,
The bull took one look and lowered his horns
And flung Billy up in the air.

The children watched in amazement
As Billy shouted, 'Get him away!'
They turned their heads and walked to the bus
And left the bull to play.

1. Think about the poem you have read and fill in the following details.

a. Who is the main character? ______________________________

b. Where is the setting of this story? ______________________________

c. What is his main fault or weakness? ______________________________

d. What happened to him? ______________________________

____

2. Write two examples of each of the following from *Billy the Bully*.

a. Active verbs ______________________

____

____

b. Direct speech ______________________

____

____

c. Rhyming words ______________________

____

____

Did you know ?

The poem 'Billy the Bully' is a form of narrative called a **cautionary tale**. It describes what happens to someone or something as a result of their actions.

Such poems are ideal to read aloud to others because they usually have:

- Active verbs
- Direct speech
- Rhyming words

Understanding Narratives

A narrative text tells an imaginary story although the story may be based on facts. *Billy the Bully* is a narrative text written in the form of a poem. The purpose of a narrative is to entertain the reader.

Types of Narrative

- short stories
- fables
- modern fantasy
- folk tales
- plays
- legends
- myths
- poems

Features of Narratives

Examples from the model text

- **Orientation**
  This is the beginning of a narrative text. It sets the mood of the story by defining the place, time, main character/s and other information to give the reader an 'orientation' or starting point.

  Billy was a bully
  The worst in all the school

- **Sequence of Events**
  This is the main body of the story. It describes an event or a sequence of events which leads the character/s into a complication where the normal events are overcome by some form of conflict. There may be more than one complication and this serves to frustrate the character/s in achieving their desired outcome. It also builds tension and anticipation in the reader.

  He teased...
  Then a dreadful thing...
  Billy jumped right over...

- **Resolution**
  Everything ends up 'happily ever after' after the conflicts are resolved. In some narratives, the resolution may be left for the reader to decide. Yet, in some narratives the resolution may not be a happy ending. For example, in this cautionary tale, the unpleasant ending is the result of someone's faults or weaknesses.

  ...and left the bull to play.

Now Get Going

When you write a cautionary tale, you must plan the story carefully. Think of all the villains you have read about over the years and write a poem on one of them. Make notes in the space below.

Checklist for your cautionary tale

1. Define your main characters clearly. ☐
2. Write in the past tense – the story has already happened! ☐
3. Use rhyming words, e.g. *much bigger than the* ***rest****... he really was a* ***pest****...* ☐
4. Use direct speech. e.g.*'Billy you're a bully...'* ☐
5. Use action verbs and feeling verbs to provide excitement and emotion, e.g.*terrorized, jumped, flung.* ☐
6. Give a title to your poem. ☐
7. Check the spelling and punctuation marks used in your writing. ☐

Who is the villian? ______________________

____

Setting ______________________

____

____

His/Her fault or weakness ______________________

____

____

____

____

____

What happened to him/her?

(This relates to his/her weakness, for example, a greedy child falls into a chocolate mould and gets eaten.)

____

____

____

____

____

____

____

____

Result of his/her weakness

____

____

____

____

Now write your poem using the notes you made. When you have finished, read it aloud to a classmate and edit the poem where necessary.

UNIT 13

TEXT TYPE: Exposition

The Skateboard Park

Sam Skateman
16B Longview Drive
Treewood

10 August 2003

The Editor
The New Bulletin
2 Pineapple Avenue
Treewood

Dear Editor

I am writing to appeal to the Town Council to review the proposed closure of the local skateboard park. Many of my friends and I were very upset to read of the news in a recent newspaper report.

The skateboard park is enjoyed by children and teenagers after school and on weekends. It is also welcomed as a popular pastime on holidays. Along with my friends, I have also made many new friends through going to the park.

Before the park was opened, there were limited places to skate. Consequently, we used our driveways, the road, footpaths, carparks and shopping centres. Some of these places prohibited skating because of potential danger to both the public and skaters. On the other hand, the park provides a safe place to skate. The ramps, humps and hills are specially designed – a lot safer than the homemade variety.

Finally, I hope this letter will prompt other young people to appeal against the closure of such a popular place in our community.

Yours sincerely,
Sam Skateman

1. Sam wrote this letter to the editor of a local newspaper. Briefly list the reasons Sam gave in protest against the closure of the skateboard park. ____________________

____

____

____

2. What do you think is Sam's weakest reason or argument? ____________________

____

3. In note form, add two more reasons that Sam could have included to make his argument stronger.

____

____

4. After reading the letter, would you support Sam's view? Why?

____

____

Understanding Expositions

An exposition explores and evaluates an issue. It presents arguments for and against the issue to convince the reader of a position. However, some expositions present only one point of view, such as Sam Skateman's letter in this unit. His aim is to appeal against the Town Council's decision to close the skateboard park. Similarly, when used in an advertisement, the exposition takes only one point of view as the argument against will defeat the purpose of persuading people to buy the product.

An exposition relies on the logical presentation of reasons and supporting facts aimed at:

- convincing the reader of the writer's point of view;
- presenting the pros and cons of an issue in order to convince the reader of the writer's point of view; and
- presenting the pros and cons of an issue to allow the reader to reach a logical conclusion.

Types of Exposition

- reviews
- debates
- speeches
- advertisements

Features of Expositions

Features of Expositions	*Examples from the model text*
• **Introduction** The introduction presents the issue in the form of an opening statement or headline.	*I am writing to protest...*
• **Argument** The arguments for and against the issue are presented, with the arguments for the issue presented first.	*The skateboard park is enjoyed by...* *Before the park was opened ...* *... the park provides a safe place ...*
• **Conclusion** The writer may draw a conclusion or restate his or her position to assist the reader in making up their mind.	*I hope this letter will prompt...*

Now Get Going

Imagine you are a Town Council member writing a letter to the editor to explain the reasons for the proposed closure of the park. Consider reasons such as complaints about noise from nearby residents, the amount of rubbish in the park, vandalism, the cost of upkeep, etc. Make notes for your argument in the space below.

Opening statement ______________________________

____

Argument ______________________________

____

____

____

____

____

____

____

____

____

____

____

Conclusion ______________________________

____

____

Checklist for your persuasive letter

1. Begin your letter by stating the issue clearly. ☐
2. Present your argument clearly, using new paragraphs for each point with supporting facts. ☐
3. Use connectors to develop your argument, e.g. *consequently, because of, on the other hand.* ☐
4. Conclude your letter by summing up your points. ☐
5. Check the spelling and punctuation marks used in your letter. ☐

Now write your letter here.

TEXT TYPE:
Personal
Recount

Tessie

We were moving house and Dad asked me to help him sort out all the boxes in the storeroom. I hadn't been in the storeroom for ages and wondered what we would find. One wall was lined with shelves, stacked with boxes almost to the ceiling. There were many other wrapped up objects of different shapes and sizes. Dad opened the boxes and rummaged through them. I moved over to a wooden box and was just about to lift the lid when it toppled over. Everything fell out into a heap.

'Be careful!' shouted Dad. 'There may be something fragile in there.'

Then I saw it! My heart began to pound and my knees began to shake. It was a rubber ring. It had belonged to my beloved dog, Tessie. She died two years ago.

I was only four when we got Tessie. I chose her from among other puppies. She was my best friend. Although she had a basket in the kitchen she would creep up to my room at night and sleep at the bottom of the bed. If I was cold she would snuggle up next to me.

Tessie could do anything. She could beg and sit and shake a paw. I taught her to fetch things.One Christmas I bought her a rubber ring. I wrapped it up in shiny paper and place it under the Christmas tree. She played with it every day. Tessie would wait at the front door when she knew it was time for me to come home from school. She would lie there panting with the rubber ring in front of her. If I didn't play, she would howl and wouldn't stop until I did. In the weekends we would take the ring to the playground and play for hours and hours until neither of us could run any more.

Then one day Tessie fell ill. She didn't wait for me by the front door any more and she didn't want to play with the ring! I tried to encourage her, 'Come on, Tessie. Come and play.'

Tessie seemed out of breath. She couldn't walk very well and she wasn't eating properly. Mum and I took her to the vet. The vet shook her head and told us that Tessie was really sick.

'There's nothing they can do for her,' Mum whispered to me.

I went to the room where Tessie was waiting and said my goodbyes. I felt her warm fur for the last time on my face and then I ran outside and cried ...

'What's the matter, son?' asked Dad. He put an arm around my shoulders.

'We all miss her,' said Dad sadly. 'She was a good dog, a really good dog.'

I nodded and put the ring back in the box.

1. What caused the boy to have a flashback? ______________________

____

____

2. What happened in the flashback? ______________________

____

____

3. What brought the boy back to the present day? ______________________

____

____

Did you know ?

A **flashback** is a story within a story. It goes back in time.

Understanding Recounts

A recount is a piece of writing that tells what has happened in the time order that it happened. There are different forms of recount:

- **Personal recount** This is a piece of writing outlining a writer's personal experience. The story of *Tessie* in this unit is a personal recount of a boy's experience. Note that there is a story within the story of *Tessie*, and this is called a 'flashback'.
- **Factual recount** This retells an event that has actually happened.
- **Imaginative recount** This tells an imaginary event.

Types of Recount

- diaries
- journals
- biographies
- autobiographies
- newspaper reports
- incident reports
- letters
- historical accounts

Features of Recounts

	Examples from the model text
• Setting A recount begins with a setting that tells the who, when, where and why of the recount.	*We were moving house and Dad ...*
• Sequence of Events The events of the recount are presented in chronological order and the writer may comment on any of the events.	*I moved over...* *Then I saw it...* *I was only four when I...*
• Conclusion This is a concluding comment where the writer provides an opinion of what has happened in the recount or a response to it.	*I nodded and put the ring back in the box.*

Now Get Going

Think of an experience that includes a flashback about a toy or other object that you find after a long time. Imagine that it holds very special memories for you — happy or sad. First, make some notes by answering the questions below.

Checklist for your personal recount

1. Define your setting clearly: the who, when, where and why of the experience. ☐
2. Arrange events in the order they happened to make the progression clear to the reader. ☐
3. Include a flashback in your recount. ☐
4. Use connectors to help the reader understand the passing of time, e.g. *She died two years ago, One Christmas, Then one day.* ☐
5. Use the first person pronouns. ☐
6. Use action verbs and feeling verbs to provide excitement and emotion, e.g. *Be careful!, shouted, pushed.* ☐
7. Write a concluding comment about the experience. ☐
8. Check the spelling and punctuation marks used in your recount. ☐

Where were you?
(grandparents' house, a relative's house)

____

What were you doing? ______________________________

____

What was the toy or object? ______________________________

____

What special memory did it bring back to you? (Say how old you were and the feelings you had.)

____

____

____

What happened to bring you back to the present day? (someone called or informed you.)

____

____

Now use your notes to write a personal recount of that experience.

UNIT 15

My Hobby

TEXT TYPE: Information Report

My hobby is finding out about Ancient Egypt. I became interested in Egypt two years ago when my grandma went there for her holidays. She sent me two postcards. One is of the sphinx, a large cat-like creature who guards the pyramids in Cairo. (Show to class.) The other one is of the River Nile. (Show to class.) My grandma brought me some papyrus, which is paper made from a plant known by the same name, that grows in Egypt. (Show to class.) She also brought me a scarab beetle from her holidays. (Show to class.) It is supposed to bring good luck.

I went to the library to find out more about the Egyptians. I found out that they buried their pharaohs in pyramids. The most famous pyramids are those in Cairo. (Show to class.) From the picture it looks as if the pyramids are surrounded by desert, but they aren't; they are in the middle of the city. I found out about the Egyptian writing called hieroglyphics, which uses pictures to form words. (Show to class.)

Mum and Dad bought me a book on Egyptian crafts for my birthday. I have made lots of things from the book, among them a Tutankhamen mask. (Show to class.) Tutankhamen was a famous boy king. I have also made an Egyptian necklace. (Show to class.) The ancient Egyptians liked wearing jewellery.

I have been to the museum in Lanchester and seen lots of Egyptian artefacts that have been dug up by archaeologists. The best thing I saw was a mummy in a coffin. I bought some pictures of what I saw at the museum. (Show to class.)

I hope to go to Egypt one day. When I am older I would like to become an archaeologist and find Egyptian treasures which have been hidden for thousands of years.

1. The students in Angela's class were asked to speak about their favourite hobby. Write three words that Angela used in describing things in Egypt.

2. What tells you that the passage above is a speech?

____

____

____

3. Why do you think Angela chose to show objects as part of her speech?

____

____

____

4. Complete Angela's notes below.

Ancient Egypt

Grandma *postcards – R. Nile and sphinx (show), beetle – good luck (show)*

Library ____

____

____

Craft Book ____

____

____

Museum ____

____

____

Did you know ?

To speak about her favourite hobby, Angela had to make notes listing cues for the speech and not read word-for-word from a sheet.

Notes for a speech should be **short** and **simple**, and should include **headings**, **keywords** and **abbreviations**.

Understanding Information Reports

An information report is a text type which presents information about a person, an object, or a place. *My Hobby* is an information report written as a speech, giving information about the country of Egypt.

Types of Information Report

- reference articles
- scientific articles
- reports
- text books
- speeches
- lectures

Although reports such as newspaper or eyewitness reports are often identified as information reports, they are more accurately described as recounts as they retell incidents that have happened.

Features of Information Reports

Examples from the model text

- **Classification**
  The opening statement classifies the subject of the report.
  My hobby is finding out about Egypt...
- **Description**
  This describes the various aspects of the topic in varying levels of detail.
  Papyrus is...
  I found out that they buried...
- **Conclusion**
  A concluding comment can complete a report but it may not always be the case.
  I hope to go to Egypt one day...

Now Get Going

Now write your own notes for a speech about your favourite hobby. Set out your notes like those on page 63 with cues to help you deliver your speech.

Checklist for your speech

1. Choose vocabulary related to the subject of your hobby e.g. *sphinx*, *River Nile*, *papyrus*. ☐
2. Use the present tense to state facts e.g. *famous pyramids are those in Egypt....* ☐
3. Use paragraphs to show separate sections in your report. ☐
4. Insert cues at appropriate points, e.g. *(Show to class)*. ☐
5. Check the spelling and punctuation marks used in your writing. ☐

Title: ______________________

Now write out the full speech about your favourite hobby.

UNIT 16

TEXT TYPE: Exposition

Does Santa Claus Exist?

Michael received this letter from his pen pal, Robert Jones.

Michael Lee
6A Orchard Street
Garden City 72700

1 April 2002

24 Robin Road
Snow Town
North Pole SNO 4RH

Dear Michael,

I am writing to tell you Santa Claus does not exist!

I know there isn't a Santa Claus because I saw my mum wrap my presents the other night. Then I watched her hide them under the bed.

I also found a red cloak, beard and hat in the wardrobe, so I know it is my dad who dresses up as Santa Claus on Christmas Eve.

I do not believe Santa Claus sent me a letter either because the handwriting was identical to my dad's.

I am sorry about this, but I thought you should know.

Yours sincerely

Robert Jones

1. Do you think Michael would believe Robert? Why?

2. What proof does Robert give to persuade Michael there isn't a Santa Claus?

3. For each piece of proof Robert gives, write an alternative explanation that proves Santa Claus **does** exist.

Proof	Alternative Explanation

Understanding Expositions

An exposition explores and evaluates an issue. It presents arguments for and against the issue to convince the reader of the writer's position. In this unit, Robert Jones has presented his point of view in the form of a letter to his pen pal.

An exposition relies on the logical presentation of facts and can be written:
- to persuade the reader of the writer's point of view;
- to present the pros and cons of an issue in order to convince the reader of the writer's point of view; and
- to present the pros and cons of an issue to allow the reader to reach a logical conclusion.

Note that when used in an advertisement, the exposition presents only one point of view as the argument against will not serve the purpose of convincing people to buy the product.

Types of Exposition

- reviews
- debates
- speeches
- advertisements

Features of Expositions

Features	*Examples from the model text*
• **Introduction** The introduction presents the issue in the form of an opening statement or headline.	*I am writing to tell you...*
• **Argument** The arguments for and against the issue are presented, with the arguments for the issue presented first.	*I know there isn't a Santa Claus...* *I also found a...*
• **Conclusion** The writer may draw a conclusion or restate his or her position to assist the reader in making up their mind.	*I am sorry about this, but...*

Now Get Going

Make notes for a letter to persuade Robert that there is a Santa Claus. You may refer to the alternative explanations you gave for Question 3.

Checklist for your persuasive letter

1. Write your address, Robert's address and the date in the correct places. ☐
2. Include an opening statement, e.g. *I am writing to tell....* ☐
3. Present your arguments clearly with each supporting reason in a separate paragraph. ☐
4. Use connectors to develop your arguments, e.g. *therefore, for example, because of.* ☐
5. Tense must suit the situation and can vary according to the issue. ☐
6. Restate your position in a concluding paragraph. ☐
7. Check the spelling and punctuation marks used in your letter. ☐

My Argument: SANTA CLAUS DOES EXIST

1. ______________________________

2. ______________________________

3. ______________________________

4. ______________________________

5. ______________________________

Now use your notes to write the letter to Robert Jones.

UNIT 17

Messages and Mummies

TEXT TYPE: Information Report

In this sequel to her ***Myths and Monsters***, Diana Parker accompanies David Hunter on his travels to Egypt to unravel the mystery set by his grandfather:

"*...Although it was long past midnight, there were people on the streets. Children my age chased after one another on the pavement while teenaged boys played football nearby. Some men wearing long robes and turbans lay fast asleep under the trees. Market traders sold fruit and vegetables from carts parked by the roadside. Mingled with the noisy traffic were wagons carrying cows and chickens. Two scruffy dogs chased a Mercedes taxi down a side street. This was Egypt!...*

...Only one more question to go, and I would have the answer – the answer which would give me the key to my grandfather's chest...."

★ History to be enjoyed
★ Puzzles to be solved
★ Mystery after mystery to be unravelled

A delightful book for boys and girls. Beautifully written.
– Children's Weekly –

I couldn't put the book down until I'd solved the puzzle. Fun from start to finish.
– Joyce Barnett (author) –

Sensitivity and humour go hand in hand with facts and accurate information.
– Children's Museum –

1. Put a tick against the features that apply to the blurb, and give an example of each.

a. ☐ Quotation from a reviewer

____

b. ☐ Quotation from the book

____

c. ☐ Information about the author

____

d. ☐ Other books written by the author

____

Did you know ?

You would find a piece of writing like this on the back cover of a book. It is called a **synopsis** or **blurb**. It usually contains information and features to make people want to read the book.

2. Who is this novel aimed at? How do you know?

____

____

____

3. What is this book about?

____

____

4. Would this blurb make you want to read the book? Why?

____

____

____

Understanding Information Reports

An information report is a text type which presents information about a person, thing or place. In this unit, the report is a blurb written in an abbreviated form as is usually seen on the back of a book jacket or cover.

Types of Information Report

- reference articles
- text books
- lectures
- synopses
- scientific articles
- blurbs

Although newspaper or eyewitness reports are often identified as information reports, they are more accurately described as recounts because they retell something that has actually happened.

Features of Information Reports

Examples from the model text

- **Classification**
  This opening statement classifies the subject of the report. — *In this sequel...*
- **Description**
  This describes the various aspects of the topic covered in the report in varying levels of detail. — *...This was Egypt! History to be enjoyed.*
- **Conclusion**
  A concluding comment can complete a report, but this may not always be the case. In the blurb, the testimonials about the book take the role of a concluding comment. — *'I couldn't put the book down...'*

Now Get Going

Look at more examples of blurbs on the back covers of other books. Choose a book you have read and write your own blurb for it. Make some notes first in the space below.

Checklist for your blurb of a book

1. Highlight the important information or features of the book. ☐
2. Use language related to the topic of the book, e.g. *market traders, unravel the mystery.* ☐
3. Use abbreviated form to excite the reader enough to want to read the book, e.g. *History to be enjoyed, Fun from start to finish.* ☐
4. Include quotations by reviewers or other authors. ☐
5. Check the spelling and punctuation marks used in the blurb. ☐

Title ______________________________

____

Author ______________________________

Information / Features ______________________________

____

____

____

____

____

Conclusion / (Quotations) ______________________________

____

____

Now use your notes to write the blurb for a book you have read.

UNIT 18

TEXT TYPE:
Information Report
(Brochure)

Visit Wales

Come to WALES

a land of high mountains and lush green valleys

- Have a holiday of a lifetime in Wales.
- It has lots to offer to families and single people, young and old alike.
- Spring, summer, autumn or winter, there's plenty on offer and plenty to do

HISTORY

Visit Caernarfon Castle or Cardiff Castle – history on your doorstep.

HILLS & VALLEYS

Follow the paths up Snowdon, the highest mountain in Wales, for magnificent views.

Visit the Swallow Falls, just one look will take your breath away.

Take the cable car up the Great Orme in Llandudno and return on the tram that slowly works its way down the mountain side.

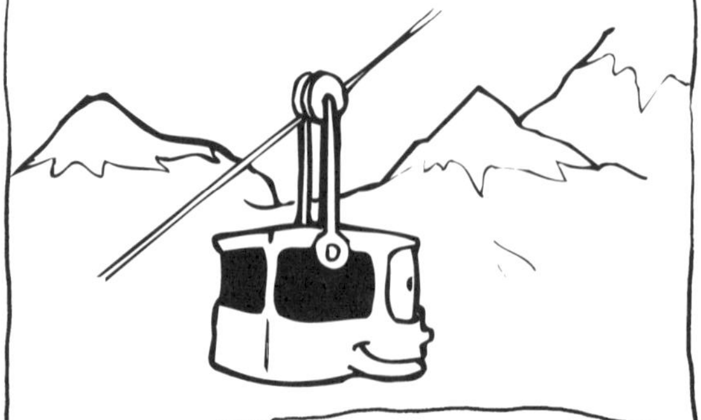

Did you know ?

Wales is one of the countries that make up the British Isles. This is a travel brochure produced by the Welsh Tourist Board.

FOOD

Try Welsh rarebit, tasty and filling, or fresh fish in one of our seaside restaurants.

SEASIDE

Miles and miles of sandy beach from Rhyl in the north to Tenby Bay in the south. The cleanest waters in the country.

Get here by car, train, bus or even bicycle – the choice is yours! Don't wait any longer!

Call us now:

☎ 44-29-75006977

Or visit our website:

www.visitwales.co.uk

1. What is the writer trying to do ?

____

2. Who is the audience of this brochure?

____

3. Does the writer achieve what he/she has set out to do?

____

4. **a.** How could the writer improve what he/she has written?

____

b. What else could the writer have said?

____

____

Understanding Information Reports

An information report is a text type which presents information about a person, thing or place. In this unit, the report is written in the form of a brochure.

Types of Information Report

- reference articles
- travel brochures
- lectures
- scientific articles
- textbooks

Note that reports such as newspaper or eyewitness reports are often identified as information reports. However, they are more accurately described as recounts because they retell something that has actually happened.

Features of Information Reports

Features of Information Reports	*Examples from the model text*
• **Classification** This opening statement classifies the subject of the report.	*Come to Wales*
• **Description** This describes the various aspects of the topic covered in the report in varying levels of detail.	*History* *Beauty*
• **Conclusion** A concluding comment can complete a report, but this may not always be the case. In the brochure, the writer concluded with an invitation to contact the Welsh Tourist Board.	*Call us now ...*

Now Get Going

Choose a country you know well or would like to know more about, and write a travel brochure on it. Imagine that your audience is a family choosing a holiday.

Checklist for your travel brochure

1. Know or research the country to ensure correct information and facts. ☐
2. Use an abbreviated form of writing, e.g. *history on your doorstep, a land of high mountains.* ☐
3. Use imperatives and lots of adjectives in the description, e.g. *visit, get here, lush green, magnificent, tasty.* ☐
4. Make good use of limited space to entice reader want to visit the country. ☐
5. Check the spelling and punctuation marks used in the brochure. ☐

Country: ______________________

Opening statement: ______________________

____

____

Description:

climate ______________________

____

____

____

other attractions ______________________

____

____

____

____

____

____

food ______________________

____

____

____

how to get there ______________________

____

____

____

Contact: ______________________

____

____

Now use the notes to design a 2-page travel brochure like the one on page 74.

Answers

Page 6–9
Unit 1 The Easter Bunny

1. Teacher check
2. Teacher check

Page 10–13
Unit 2 The School Play

1. • Jack's mum spilt too much water on the waxed floor
   • The cow slid into the beanstalk
   • The beanstalk and the giant tumbled down
   • The giant got caught in the washing line and fell off the stage
2. Teacher check
3. Teacher check

Page 14–17
Unit 3 A Landing Surprise!

1. Set in the future; the vocabulary used
2. **a.** Teacher check
   b. The active type of verbs make the story action-packed and exciting.
3. **a.** Captain Phantos, Commander Ramesh, crew, UFOs
   b. Planet Ogg and Starship *Breaker*
   c. Starship *Breaker* lands on Planet Ogg; Captain Phantos and crew embark and explore.
   d. A red mist circled the ship and then ... Boom!

Page 18–21
Unit 4 White

1. clouds, snowflakes, ice-cream, teeth, swan, skeletons, blossom, polar bear, dove
2. Teacher check
3. snowflakes – swirl and twirl
   ice-cream – cool and sweet
   teeth – small children smile
   swan – gliding gracefully
   skeletons – Halloween
   blossom – trees in the park
   polar bear – majestic and strong
   dove – sign of peace

Page 22–25
Unit 5 The Three Goats

1. **a.** The Three Little Pigs
   b. Teacher check
2. Teacher check

Page 26–29
Unit 6 Environment Week

1. The programme or plan of a trip.
2. Teacher check
3. The first one. Because it is too brief for others to understand fully.
4. The second one. Because it is clearer, has better presentation, and is more detailed.

Page 30–33
Unit 7 Crocodile on the Loose!

1. Who: crocodile, Riverton students, principal, gardener, park manager
   When: Friday lunchtime
   Where: Riverton Secondary School compound
   What: crocodile escaped from Wildlife Park and had been eating students' lunches
2. Teacher check
3. Teacher check

Page 34–37
Unit 8 The School Canteen

1. **a.** enjoy canteen lunches and going on roster
   b. saves them from always preparing lunches; feel pressured to buy lunches and to go on roster
   c. unhealthy food choices
   d. litter in school compound
   e. difficult to find volunteers for roster
2. Teacher check

Page 38–41
Unit 9 The Race

1. *The Race* has the same moral as Aesop's story.
2. Slow and steady wins the race.
3. Teacher check

Page 42–45
Unit 10 Daniel Brown

1. **a.** third person
   b. Daniel's teacher
   c. Daniel's parents and new teacher
2. *Adjectives*: good, careless, sound, satisfactory, mentally quick, careful, friendly, pleasant, new
   Adverbs: fluently, with confidence, good, well, quick, sound
3. *Conjunctions*: and, but, as, however, because, so, even though
4. *Positive adjectives/adverbs*: good, friendly, pleasant, new, fluently, with confidence, well, quick, sound
   Negative adjectives/adverbs: careless

Page 46–49
Unit 11 Hand-held Computer Games

1. Hand-held computer games should not be banned from schools.
2. Paragraph 2 – Teenagers would be unhappy and lonely.
   Paragraph 3 – Computer games don't interfere with school work.
   Paragraph 4 – They develop hand–eye coordination and are quiet.
3. Teacher check

Page 50–53
Unit 12 Billy the Bully

1. **a.** Billy
   b. school, farm
   c. being a bully
   d. attacked by a bull
2. Teacher check

Page 54–57
Unit 13 The Skateboard Park

1. The skateboard park is enjoyed by many children and teenagers in leisure hours; a place to make new friends; stopped skating in prohibited places; park is specially designed; safer than homemade ramps etc.
2. Teacher check
3. Teacher check
4. Teacher check

Page 58–61
Unit 14 Tessie

1. The rubber ring belonging to his dog
2. He remembered the time he spent with his dog before she died.
3. His father called him.

Page 62–65
Unit 15 My Hobby

1. sphinx, Cairo, papyrus, scarab, pharaohs, Tutankhamen, Nile, hieroglyphics
2. 'Show to class' is written in brackets.
3. Teacher check
4. Teacher check

Page 66–69
Unit 16 Does Santa Claus Exist?

1. Teacher check
2. He saw his mum wrap presents; he found a red cloak, beard and hat in the wardrobe, and a letter written by his dad.
3. Teacher check

Page 70–73
Unit 17 Messages and Mummies

1. **a.** yes; examples – Teacher check
   b. yes; examples – Teacher check
   c. yes; writes stories based on historical facts and information
   d. yes; Myths and Monsters
2. Boys and girls. *Clues*: '...children my age...'; David was a grandson; review in Children's Weekly
3. David has to travel around Egypt following clues given by his grandfather to find the key to his grandfather's chest.
4. Teacher check

Page 74–77
Unit 18 Visit Wales

1. The writer is trying to make people want to visit Wales.
2. People who want to go on holiday, especially adults.
3. Teacher check
4. **a.** Teacher check
   b. Teacher check